High in

By Liza Charlesworth

ISBN: 978-1-339-02794-4

Art Director: Tannaz Fassihi; Designer: Tanya Chernyak
Photos © Getty Images and Shutterstock.com.

1 2 3 4 5 6 7 8 9 10   68   32 31 30 29 28 27 26 25 24 23

Printed in Jiaxing, China. First printing, August 2023.

In a tree, you can often see jays.
But a lot of animals stay in trees.
Let's meet a few of them!

A tree is a place for frogs.
Their feet can stick to twigs.
They sit high in the treetops
and say, "Ribbit, ribbit!"

See the sloth and its cute pup.
The pup will eat, sleep,
and grow up in a tree.
It is a safe home for sloths.

Snakes can be seen in trees.
They rest and hunt for meals.
They slip, slide, and say, "Ssss!"

Do bats stay in trees? Yes!
A bat grips a branch with its feet
and naps upside down.

Insects spend a lot of time in trees.

Buzz!

They buzz, creep, and hide. Can you spot the moth resting on the tree trunk?

This ape is a gibbon.
It eats figs, twigs, and insects.
It swings and leaps in the treetops.
It thinks a tree is the place to be!